Learners

Penguins

by Annabelle Lynch

W
FRANKLIN WATTS
LONDON•SYDNEY

First published in 2014 by
Franklin Watts
338 Euston Road
London NW1 3BH

Franklin Watts Australia
Level 17/207 Kent Street
Sydney NSW 2000

Copyright © Franklin Watts 2014

Picture credits: Doug Allan/Bluegreen Pictures/
Alamy: 9. axily/Shutterstock: 6-7. BMJ/Shutterstock:
14-15. Volodymyr Goinyk/Shutterstock: front cover,
18. Anton Ivanov/Shutterstock: 4-5. Olga
Khoroshunova/Shutterstock: 10-11. Micha Klootwijk/
Dreamstime: 8. Stephan Pietzko /Dreamstime: 17.
Ronsmith/Shutterstock: 21. sunsinger/Shutterstock:
1, 13. Mogens Trolle/Shutterstock: 20.

A CIP catalogue record for this book is
available from the British Library.

Dewey number: 598.47

ISBN 978 1 4451 2912 9 (hbk)
ISBN 978 1 4451 3046 0 (pbk)
Library eBook ISBN 978 1 4451 2918 1

Series Editor: Julia Bird
Series Advisor: Catherine Glavina
Series Designer: Peter Scoulding

Printed in China

Franklin Watts is a division of Hachette Children's Books,
an Hachette UK company. www.hachette.co.uk

Contents

The words in **bold** can be found in the glossary.

What are penguins?

Penguins are a funny kind of bird. They can't fly, but they can swim! Penguins spend most of their life in the sea.

Over time, penguins' wings have turned into **flippers** to help them swim.

Where are penguins found?

Penguins live on sandy, rocky or icy **shores**.

Some penguins live in warm places, but most prefer colder seas.

Penguins live in big groups called rookeries or colonies.

Penguin food

Penguins eat fish, **squid** and tiny animals called krill.

They can dive deep under the water to catch their **prey**.

Some penguins can hold their breath for more than 20 minutes.

Fairy
penguins

Fairy penguins are the smallest penguins. They have shiny blue, grey and white feathers. They make their nests among rocks or dig holes in the sand.

Fairy penguins live on the coasts of Australia and New Zealand.

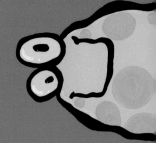

Hopping penguins

Rockhopper penguins are small but noisy! They are called rockhoppers because they like to jump from rock to rock.

Rockhoppers shake their feathers and wave their flippers to get each other's attention!

13

Emperor penguins

Emperor penguins are the biggest of all the penguins.

They live in the icy Antarctic.
In the freezing cold winters
they **huddle** in big groups
for warmth.

Emperor penguin groups move
around so that each penguin
gets a turn in the warm middle.

Yellow-eyed penguins

Yellow-eyed penguins are very **rare**. They are only found in New Zealand. Yellow-eyed penguins are shy. Their nests are hidden in thick forest.

Yellow-eyed penguins are also called hoiho penguins, which means 'the noise shouters'!

Penguin babies

Penguin babies **hatch** from eggs. The eggs are kept safe in a nest or in a **pouch** between their father's legs until they are ready to hatch.

Penguins feed their babies by passing soft food from their beak into the baby's beak.

Penguin fun

Penguins love to play! They slide around the ice on their bellies. This is called tobogganing. They also love jumping into the sea.

Tobogganing helps penguins travel a long way to find food.

Glossary

hatch – to break out from inside an egg

flipper – a flat, wide arm or leg, which helps animals to swim

huddle – to stand close together

pouch – a pocket that holds things

prey – an animal eaten by another animal

shore – where the land meets the sea

squid – a sea creature with a long, soft body

rare – something that is not often seen

Websites:

http://kids.nationalgeographic.com/kids/animals/

creaturefeature/emperor-penguin/

http://www.kidzone.ws/animals/penguins/facts6.htm

Quiz

1. What have penguins' wings turned into?

2. What are penguin groups called?

3. Which are the smallest penguins?

4. Where are emperor penguins found?

5. How do penguins feed their babies?

6. What does tobogganing help penguins to do?

The answers are on page 24

Answers

1. Flippers
2. Colonies or rookeries
3. Fairy penguins
4. In the Antarctic
5. By passing them soft food from their beaks
6. To travel a long way to find food

Index